Handwriting
Skills Workbook

This workbook belongs to

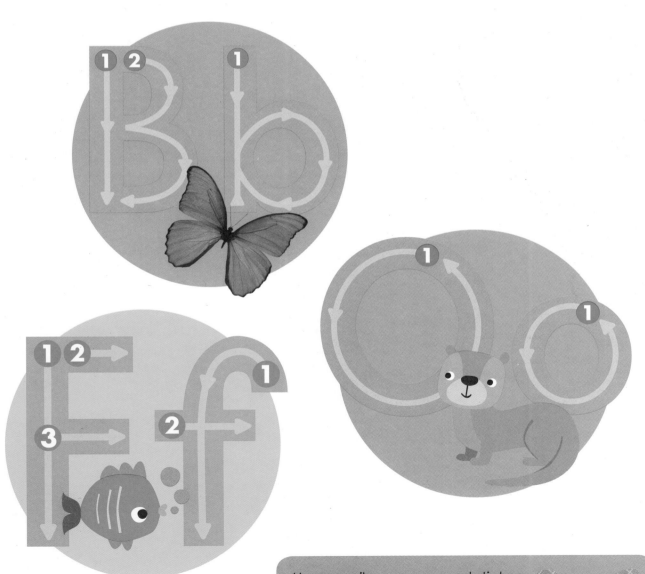

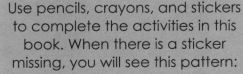

Trace the letters with your finger.

A a

apple

anchor

Trace the **a**'s.

A A A A A A A A A A

a a a a a a a a a a

Trace and write more **a**'s.

A A A

a a a

Trace the sentence.

Andy the alligator
ate apples.

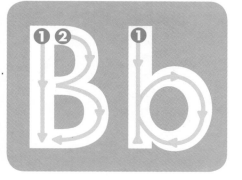

butterfly

ball

Trace the **b**'s.

Trace and write more **b**'s.

Trace the sentence.

Bella the baboon
bakes bread.

cat

car

Trace the **c**'s.

CCCCCCCC

cccccccc

Trace and write more **c**'s.

CCC

ccc

Trace the sentence.

Carl the cow
likes cupcakes.

doll

dog

Trace the **d**'s.

D D D D D D D

d d d d d d d

Trace and write more **d**'s.

D D D

d d d

Trace the sentence.

Dylan the dinosaur danced at the disco.

exercise

elephant

Trace the **e**'s.

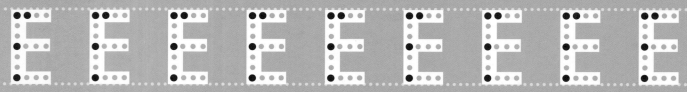

Trace and write more **e**'s.

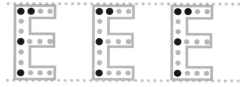

Trace the sentence.

Ellie the eagle

eats eggs.

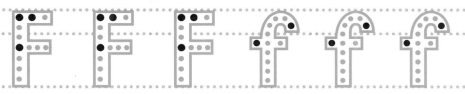

Trace and write **f**'s.

F F F f f f

F F f f

Trace the sentence.

Fay the fish has five green fins.

Trace and write **g**'s.

G G G g g g

G G g g

Trace the sentence.

Greg the gorilla gave a growl.

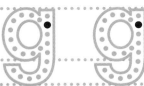

horse

house

Trace the **h**'s.

H H H H H H H H H

h h h h h h h h h

Trace and write more **h**'s.

H H H

h h h

Trace the sentence.

Holly is a hairy
hamster.

8

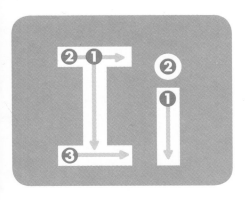

iguana

ink

Trace the **i**'s.

I I I I I I I I

i i i i i i i i i i i

Trace and write more **i**'s.

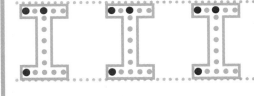

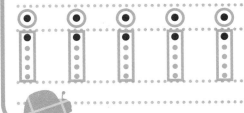

Trace the sentence.

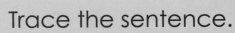

Isaac the

insect is ill.

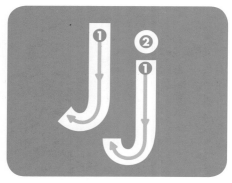

J J J j j j

j j

Trace the sentence.

Jenny the jaguar
is in the jungle.

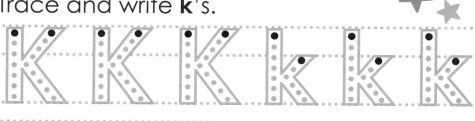

Trace and write **k**'s.

K K K k k k

K K k k

Trace the sentence.

Kyle the kitten
is kind.

L l

lamp

lion

Trace the l's.

L L L L L L L L L L L L

l l l l l l l l l l l l

Trace and write more l's.

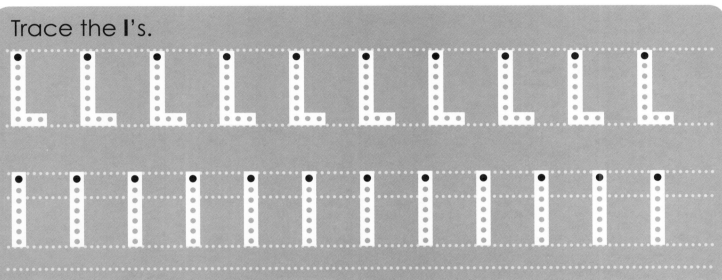

L L L

l l l

Trace the sentence.

Lily the lizard
loves lunch.

mug

monkey

Trace the **m**'s.

M M M M M M M M M M

m m m m m m m m m m

Trace and write more **m**'s.

M M M

m m m

Trace the sentence.

Matt the mouse
drinks milk.

nurse

necklace

Trace the **n**'s.

N N N N N N N

n n n n n n n n

Trace and write more **n**'s.

N N N

n n n

Trace the sentence.

Nicola the newt

needs a nap.

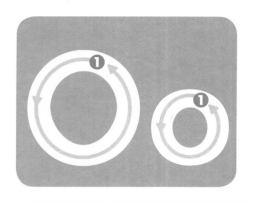

octag**o**n

ostrich

Trace the **o**'s.

Trace and write more **o**'s.

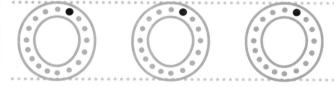

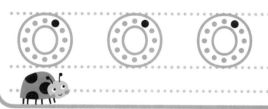

Trace the sentence.

Ollie the otter
buys oranges.

parrot

piano

Trace the **p**'s.

Trace and write more **p**'s.

Trace the sentence.

Poppy the panda
paints pretty pictures.

Trace and write **q**'s.

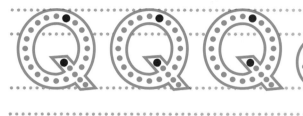

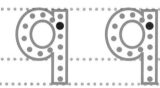

Q Q Q Q q q q

Q Q q q q

Trace the sentence.

Quincy is a quiet quail.

Trace and write **r**'s.

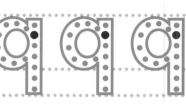

R R R R r r r

R R r r

Trace the sentence.

Ruby the rabbit runs in the rain.

snake   **sa**ndcastle

Trace the **s**'s.

Trace and write more **s**'s.

Trace the sentence.

Sam the spider
spins a web.

train

tiger

Trace the t's.

T T T T T T T T T T

t t t t t t t t t t

Trace and write more t's.

T T T

t t t

Trace the sentence.

Tara the tortoise
ate two tomatoes.

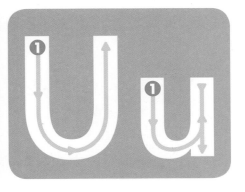

umbrella

umpire

Trace the **u**'s.

U U U U U U U U U U

u u u u u u u u u u

Trace and write more **u**'s.

U U U

U U U

Trace the sentence.

Ursula the urchin
lives underwater.

vase   **v**olcano

Trace the **v**'s.

Trace and write more **v**'s.

Trace the sentence.

Vinnie the vulture

lives in a cave.

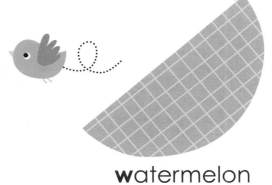

wand   **w**atermelon

Trace the **w**'s.

W W W W W W

W W W W W W

Trace and write more **w**'s.

W W W

W W W

Trace the sentence.

Willow is a
wise walrus.

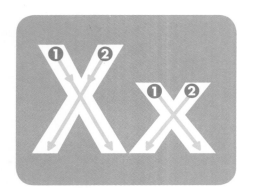

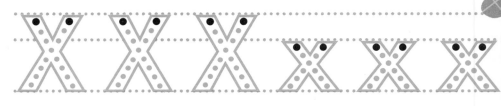

Trace and write **x**'s.

X X X X X X X X X X

X X X X

Trace the sentence.

Xander the fox
met an ox.

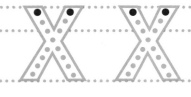

Trace and write **y**'s.

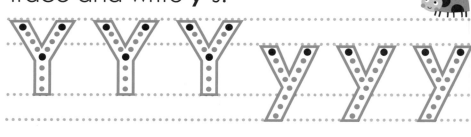

Y Y Y Y Y Y y y y y

Y Y Y y y

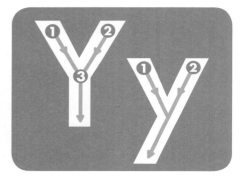

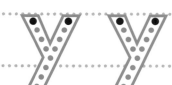

Trace the sentence.

Yasmin the
yak is yellow.

Zz

zipper   **z**oo

Trace the **z**'s.

Z Z Z Z Z Z Z Z Z

z z z z z z z z z

Trace and write more **z**'s.

Z Z Z

z z z

Trace the sentence.

Zack is a
lazy zebra.

Congratulations!

GOOD WORK AWARD!

Name: ....

has successfully completed the

Handwriting

Skills Workbook

Date: ....

Search this page for the stickers you need.

Page **3**

Pages **4–5**

Pages **6–7**

Pages **8–9**

Pages **10–11**

Pages **12–13**

Page **14**

Pages **16–17**

Pages **18–19**

Pages **20–21**

Pages **22–23**

Certificate stickers

Extra stickers